Inspiring Islamic Stories

for Boys and Girls

Volume 1

Author: Julia Hanke

Illustrator: Sarah Mahmoud

Copyright © 2020 by Julia Hanke
All rights reserved

As Salamu Alaykum, Dear Readers,

As Muslim parents, we all want one thing for our children: provide an authentic Islamic education. We want our children to grow up with good Islamic morals, manners, behavior, and values. The problem I encountered as a homeschooling mother of three children, age 8, 5, and 1 is the following: The Islamic books for children I found and bought for my children are either lacking in authenticity, are written in a language that is too complicated for children, or they hardly contain valuable content. The content is so low that my children would learn almost nothing new.

This is why I wrote this book: "Islamic Inspirational Stories."

This book provides rich content with valuable information Muslim children need to grow into pious, well-mannered, and well-behaved, kind human beings. As a holder of a Bachelor in Education and Islamic Sciences, I have learned how to make sources transparent while writing. It is this transparency that you will find in almost no other Islamic book for children.

This is what was especially important to me, so I was passionate about writing this book. From this book, your child will in sha Allah learn beautiful Islamic values from real role models like our beloved Prophet Muhammad, Prophet Moses, and others, rather than from fictional, fairy tale characters. Don't let your child miss out on essential and nurturing Islamic education. Grab a copy for your relatives and friends, and share the joy of learning!

contents

01

PROPHET MUHAMMAD (PEACE AND BLESSINGS OF ALLAH UPON HIM)

31

PROPHET MUSA ASKING TO SEE ALLAH

38

THE STORY OF THE GARDENS OF SHEBA

01

PROPHET MUHAMMAD (PEACE AND BLESSINGS OF ALLAH UPON HIM)

01

Muhammad Peace and Blessings of Allah upon him

Shaykh Muhammad ibn Ibraaheem al-Tuwayjri describes how the Arabs of the Prophet Muhammad's time prayed to statues of imaginary gods known as idols. There were idols in their homes, their markets, outside of the Ka'ba, and even inside the Kaaba. People also used to visit soothsayers and magicians to ask them for help, instead of Allah.

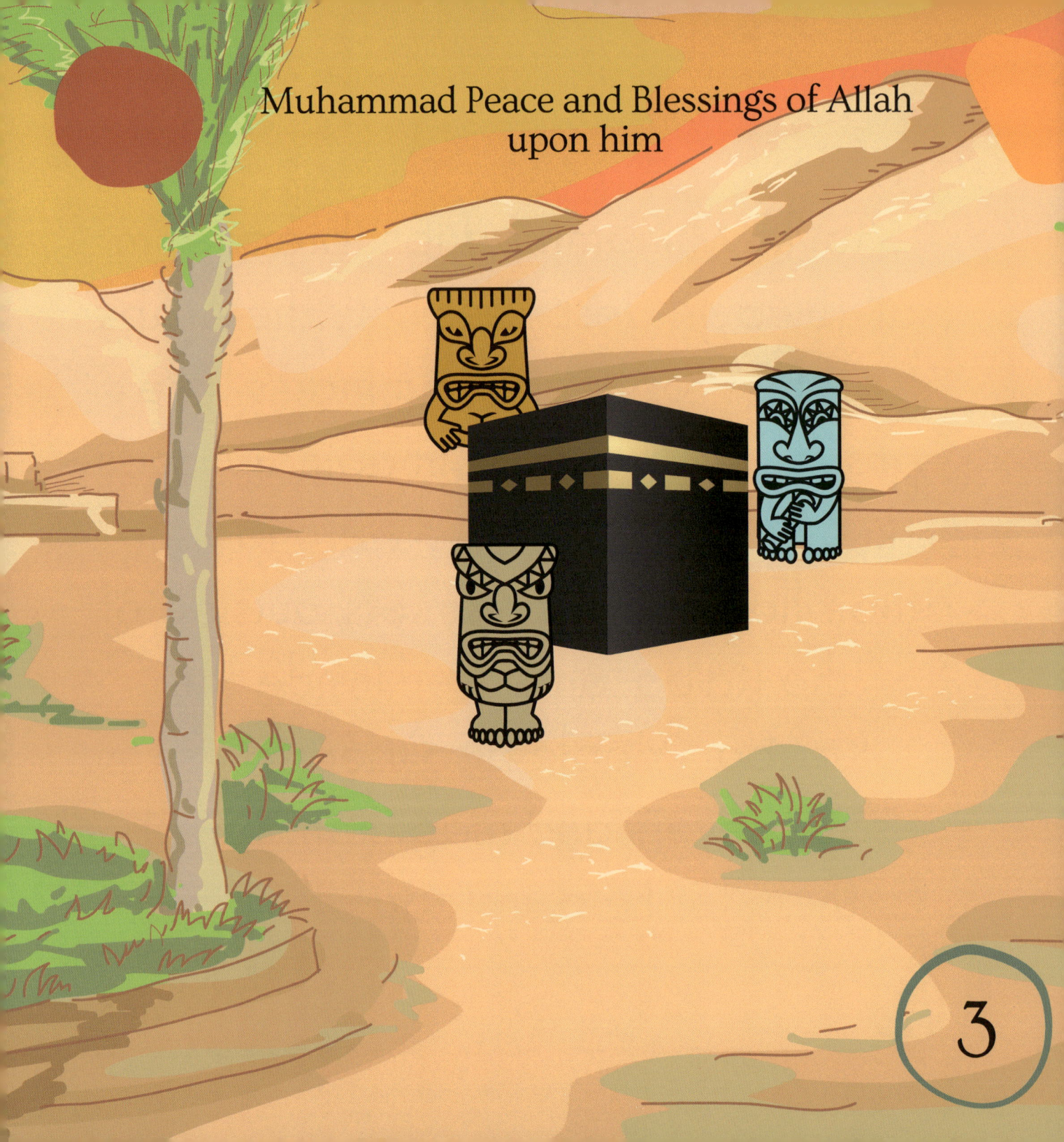

Muhammad Peace and Blessings of Allah upon him

When these kinds of shirk – which is to worship anyone other than Allah -- and evil became so widespread, Allah sent Muhammad (peace and blessings of Allah be upon him) to bring them the correct guidance and message.

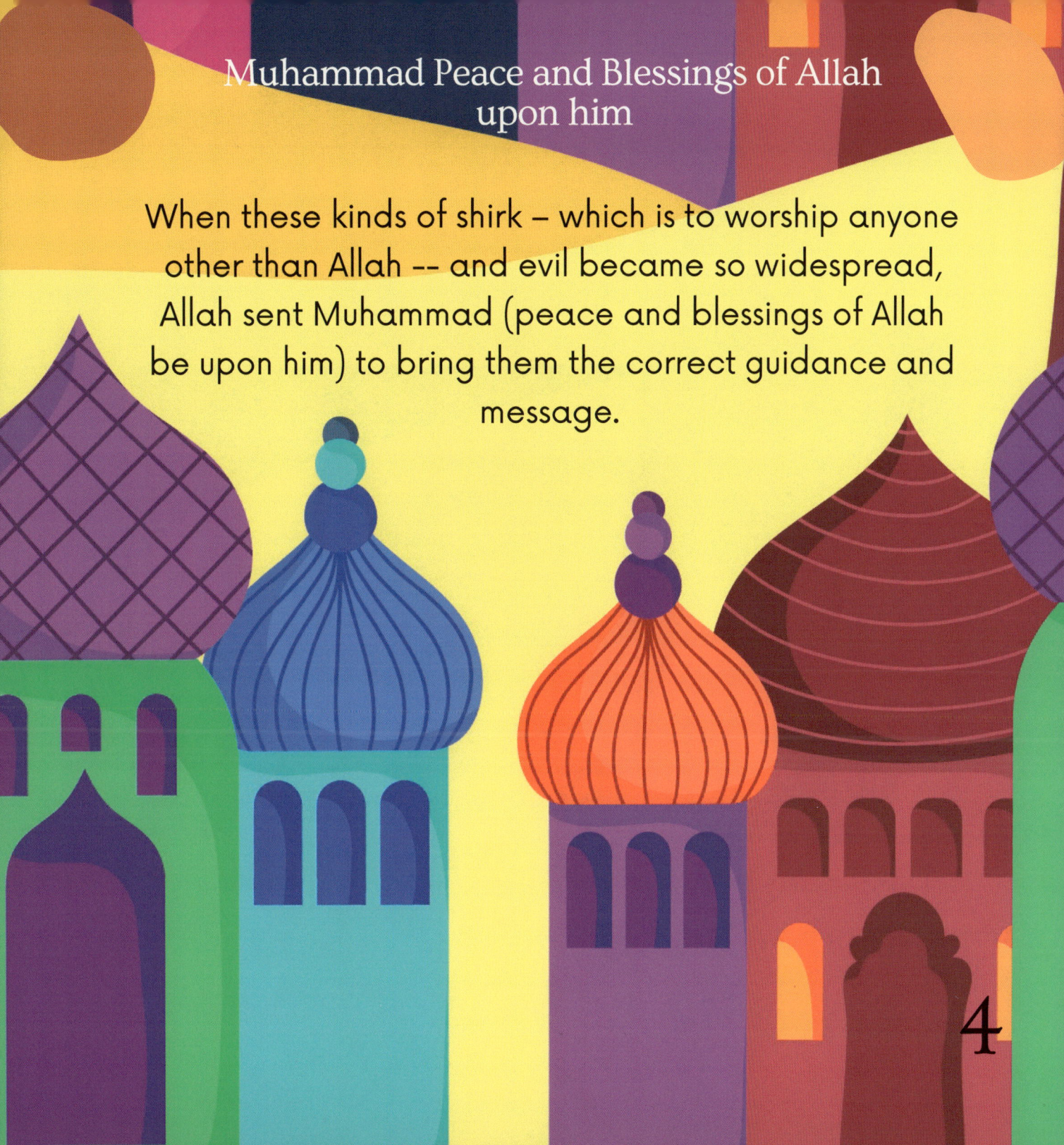

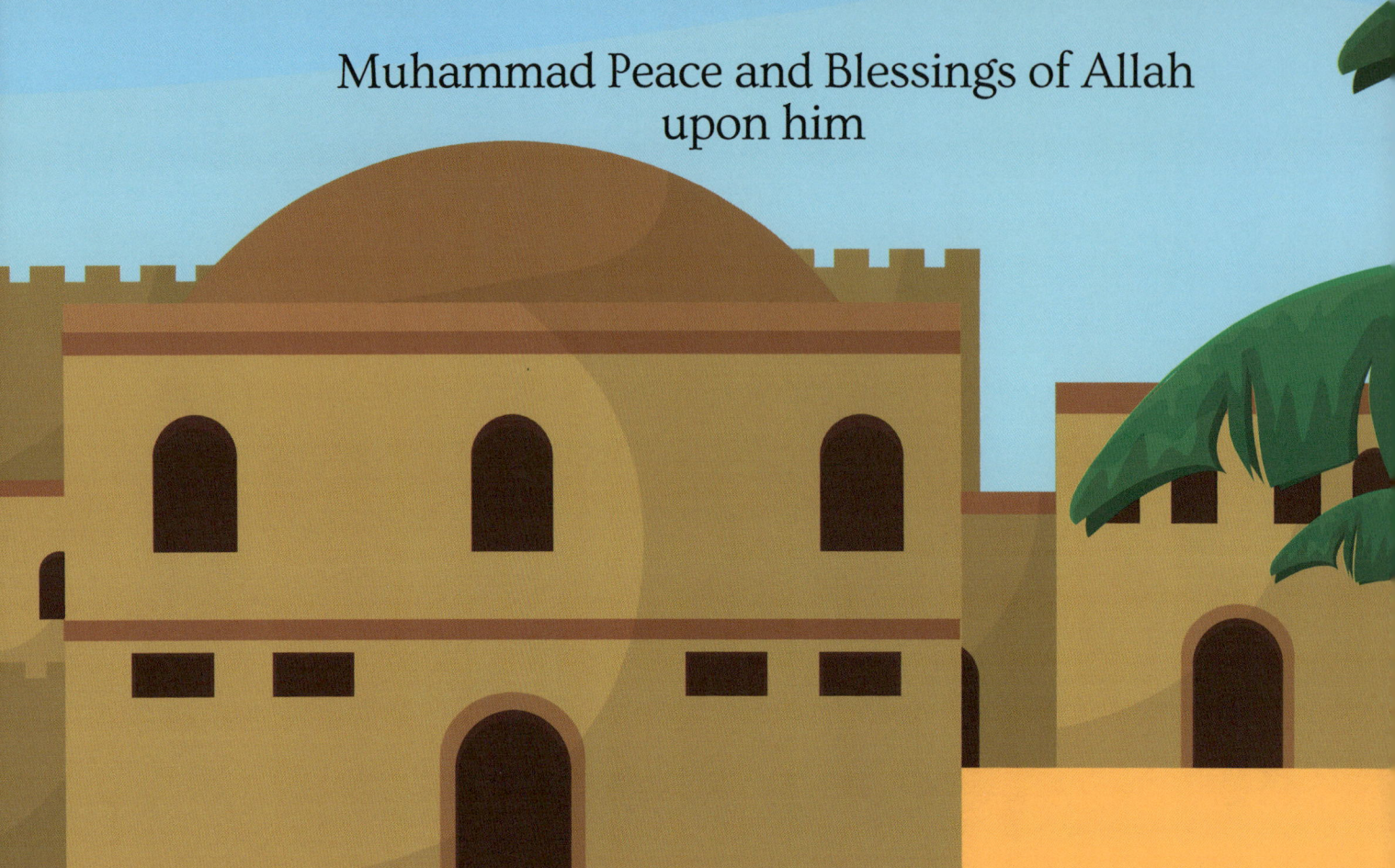

Muhammad Peace and Blessings of Allah upon him

At the age of 40, Prophet Muhammad (peace and blessings of Allah be upon him) became the last prophet of Islam, inviting people to worship Allah alone and stop praying to false idols.

Muhammad Peace and Blessings of Allah upon him

To show how powerless these statues of imaginary gods were, Prophet Muhammad (peace and blessings of Allah be upon him) and his Companions (may Allah be pleased with them) broke the statues. If they had been real gods, the statues should have been protected from being broken. But of course, they were not. They were just images of false gods made by people and were destroyed.

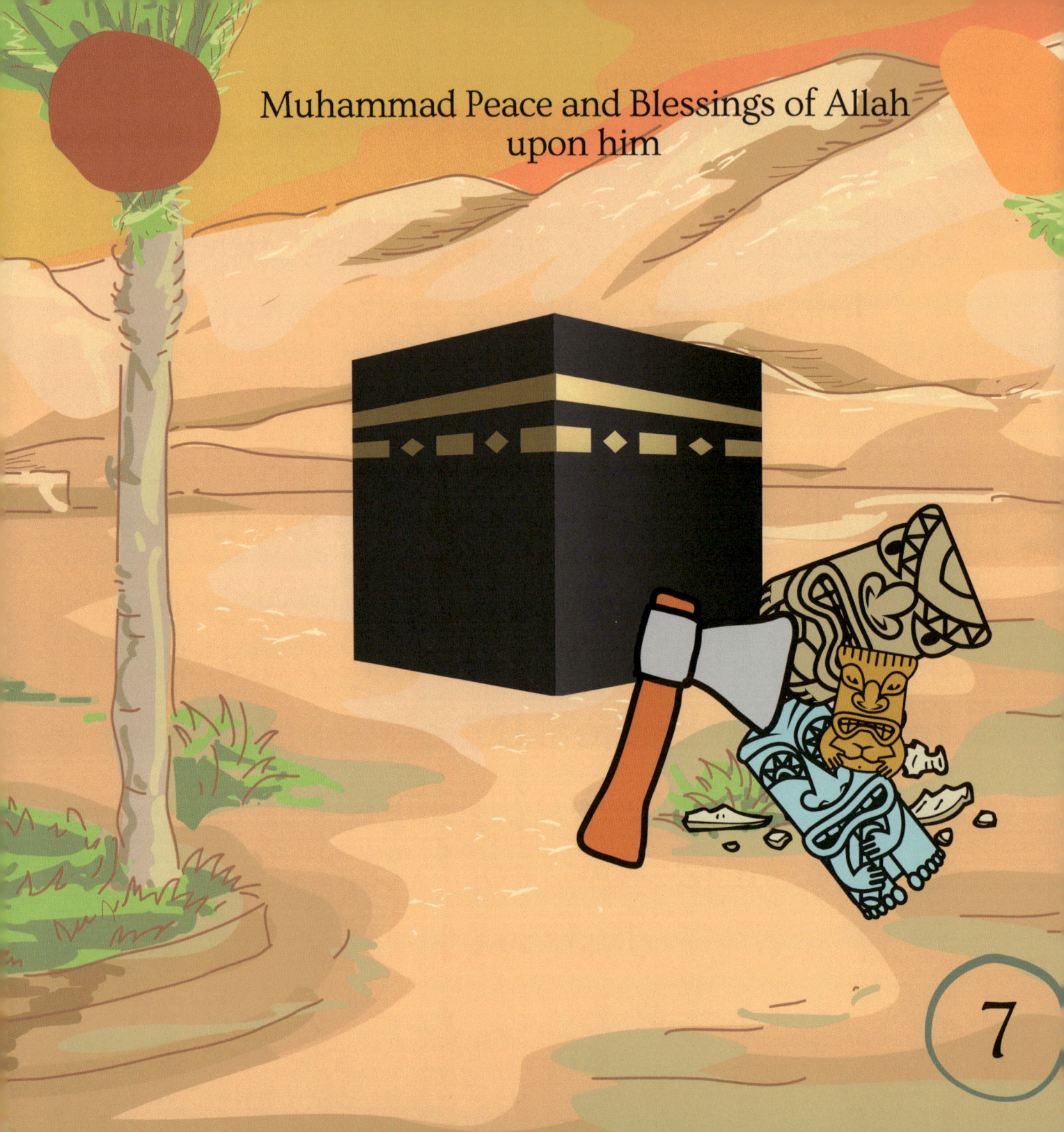

Muhammad Peace and Blessings of Allah upon him

Prophet Muhammad (peace and blessings of Allah be upon him) received the first Surah of the Quran in the cave of Hiraa', where he used to pray to Allah. The Surah was revealed to him through the angel Jibraeel, who said to him, "Read! "The Messenger (peace and blessings of Allah be upon him) did not know how to read, so he answered, "I am not a reader."

Muhammad Peace and Blessings of Allah upon him

Again, Jibraeel said, "Read," and the Prophet again said he did not know-how. The third time the angel ordered him to read, the Prophet answered with the first words of the Quran revealed to humankind:

Muhammad Peace and Blessings of Allah upon him

"Read! In the Name of your Lord Who has created (all that exists). He has created man from a clot (a piece of thick coagulated blood). Read! And your Lord is the Most Generous.
[al-'Alaq 96:1-3 – interpretation of the meaning]

Muhammad Peace and Blessings of Allah upon him

Shaykh Muhammad ibn Ibraaheem al-Tuwayjri explains that after reciting this first surah from the Quran in the cave of Hiraa', "the Messenger went back home, his heart pounding." He was overwhelmed by what had happened – the appearance of an angel and his ability to recite Allah's message known as the Quran. Shaykh Ibn Ibraaheem al-Tuwayjri continues: "At home, he saw his wife Khadijah and told her what had happened, saying, "I feared for myself."

Muhammad Peace and Blessings of Allah upon him

She calmed him down and told him Allah must have chosen him to receive the Quran because the Prophet was such a good man.

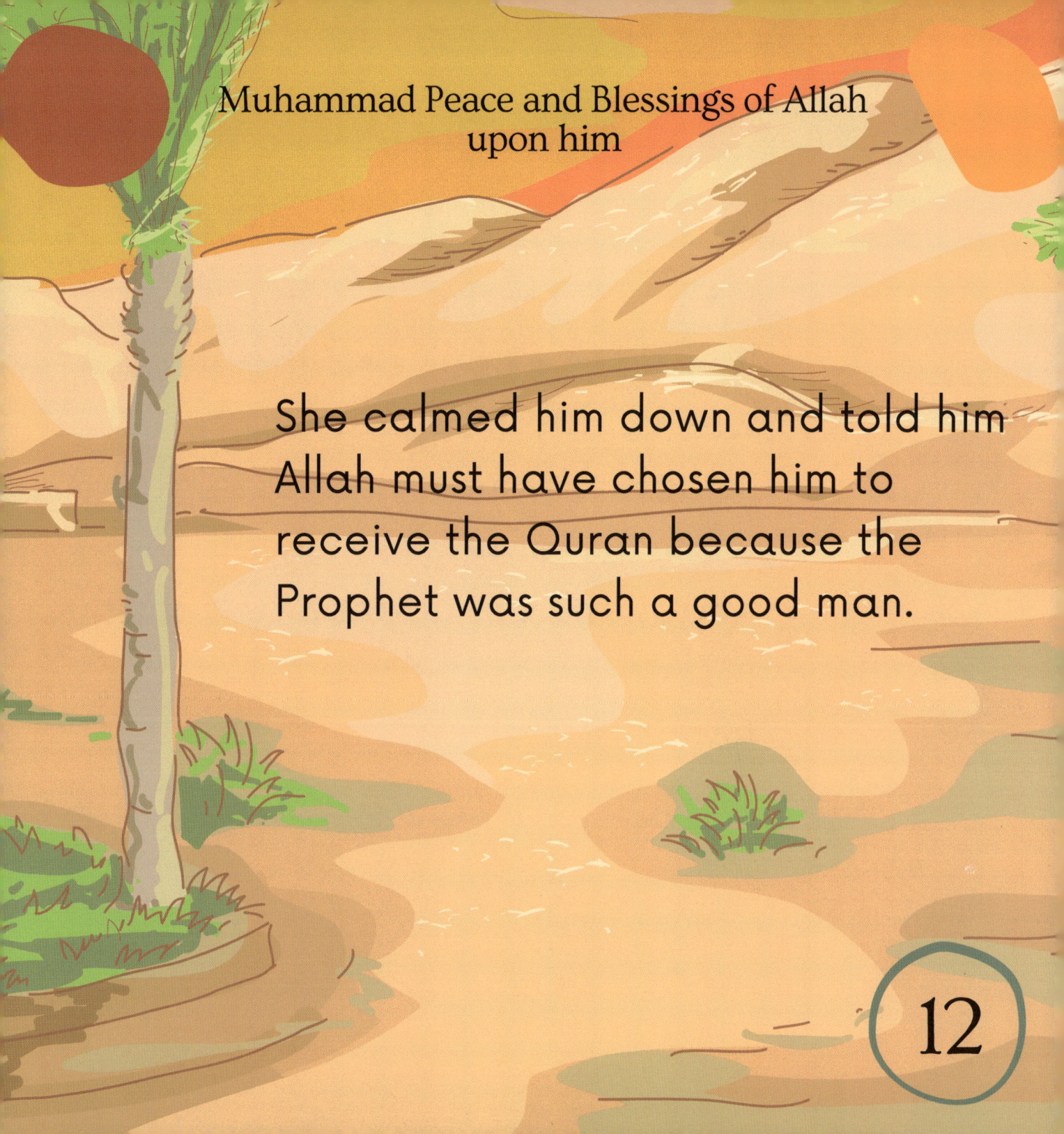

Muhammad Peace and Blessings of Allah upon him

He always visited his relatives, helped the poor and the weak, was kind to his guests, gave Sadaqah (charity), and helped when someone was unwell. Khadijah's confidence and trust in the Prophet reassured and comforted him.

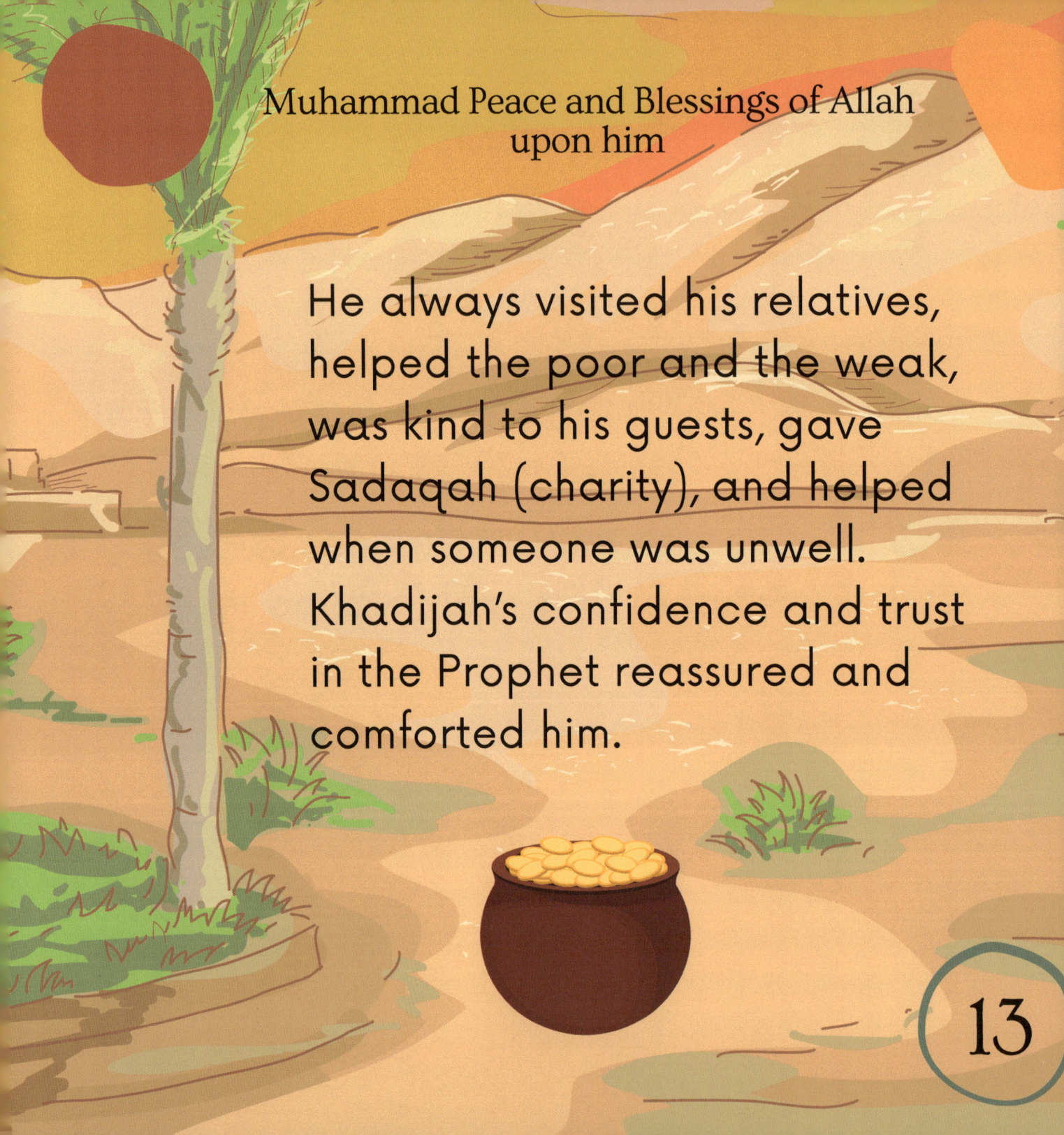

Muhammad Peace and Blessings of Allah upon him

Another day, when the Prophet was out walking, again, the angel Jibraeel came to him. The experience again shook the Prohet. He went back to his house and wrapped himself in his blanket to settle himself. Then Allah revealed the words (interpretation of the meaning): "O you (Muhammad) enveloped in garments! Arise and warn!" [al-Muddaththir 74:1-2]

Muhammad Peace and Blessings of Allah upon him

After that, more Surahs were revealed to the Prophet (peace and blessings of Allah be upon him), one after another. The Prophet stayed in Mecca for 13 years, calling the people to reject false gods and instead pray only to Allah, first in secret, and then openly, when Allah commanded him to it.

Muhammad Peace and Blessings of Allah upon him

So he called them in a gentle and kind way, without fighting or giving insult. In the beginning, only a few people believed him. These first Muslims were men and women, rich and poor, showing how the message of Islam was for all people, not just one tribe or one class.

13

Muhammad Peace and Blessings of Allah upon him

One group of people did not like the Prophet (peace and blessings of Allah be upon him). The Quraish were a family who was not Muslim and did not like Islam or its followers. They tried to catch Muslims and hurt them so they would leave Islam, sometimes even killing them.

Muhammad Peace and Blessings of Allah upon him

These early Muslims were treated so badly that some of them escaped to another country called Abyssinia, to better practice Islam.

18

Muhammad Peace and Blessings of Allah upon him

The situation was so bad that the Messenger commanded his companions to go to another city called Medina to get away from the people who were hurting them. So they left for Medina in a migration called The Hijrah.

19

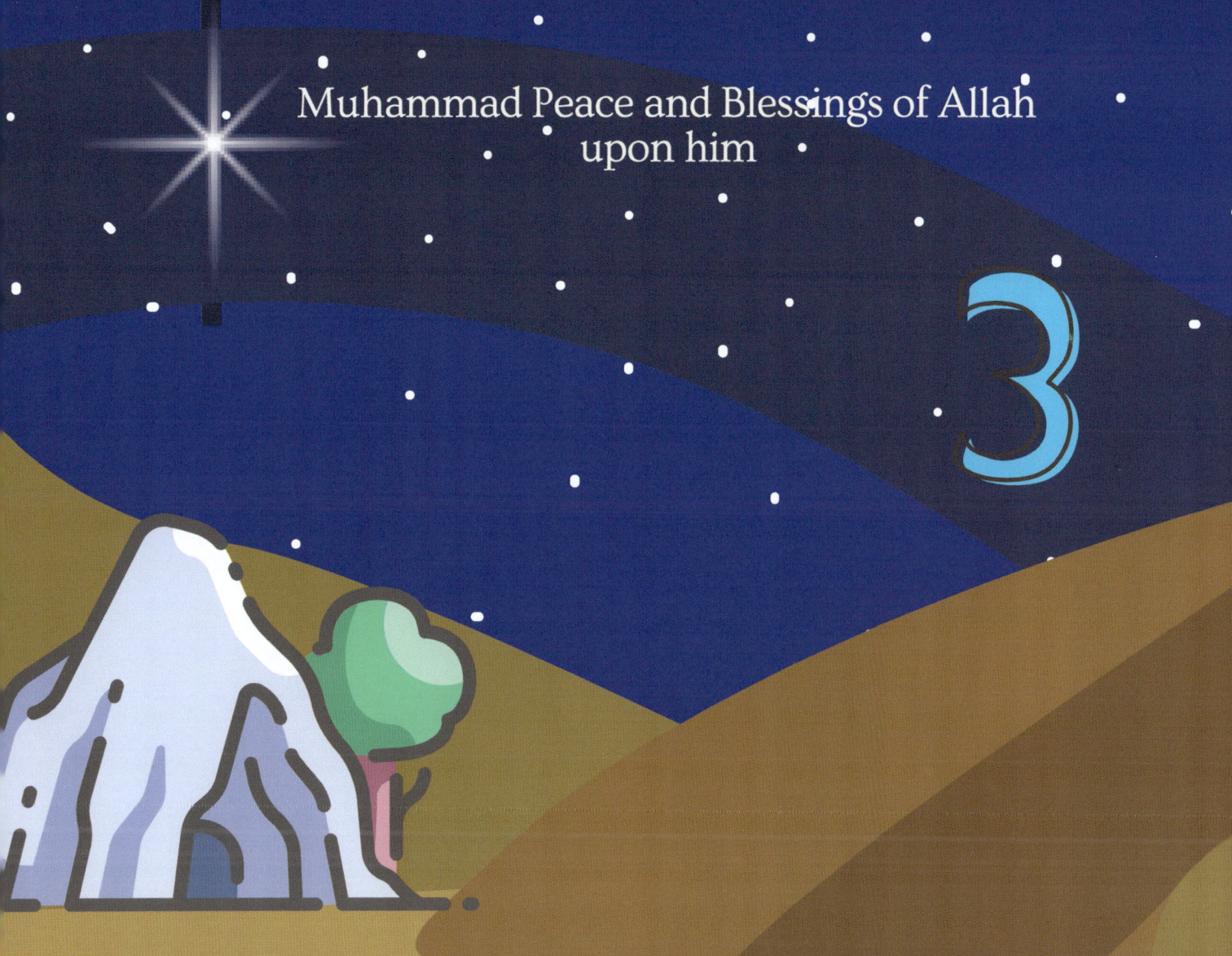

When all the other Muslims left Mecca, the Messenger of Allah and his closest friend Abu Bakr set out. On the way, they wanted to stop in the cave of Thawr and stayed there for three nights.

Muhammad Peace and Blessings of Allah upon him

The Quraish were alarmed when they left, and they looked for them everywhere. But Allah protected His Messenger. The Quraish searchers were unable to find the Prophet and Abu Bakr, and they could continue their travels safely.

21

Muhammad Peace and Blessings of Allah upon him

When the Messenger (peace and blessings of Allah be upon him) reached Medina, the Muslims who had gone there before him shouted out "Allahu akbar! Allah is the Greatest" in celebration of his arrival. Men, women, and children all came out to see him and welcome him.

Muhammad Peace and Blessings of Allah upon him

The Prophet stayed in Quba, where he and the Muslims built the first masjid of Islam – the Masjid of Quba, which still stands to this day. Afterward, they went to Medina, where they build the Masjid an-Nabawiy, known as the Mosque of the Prophet, with its famous green dome.

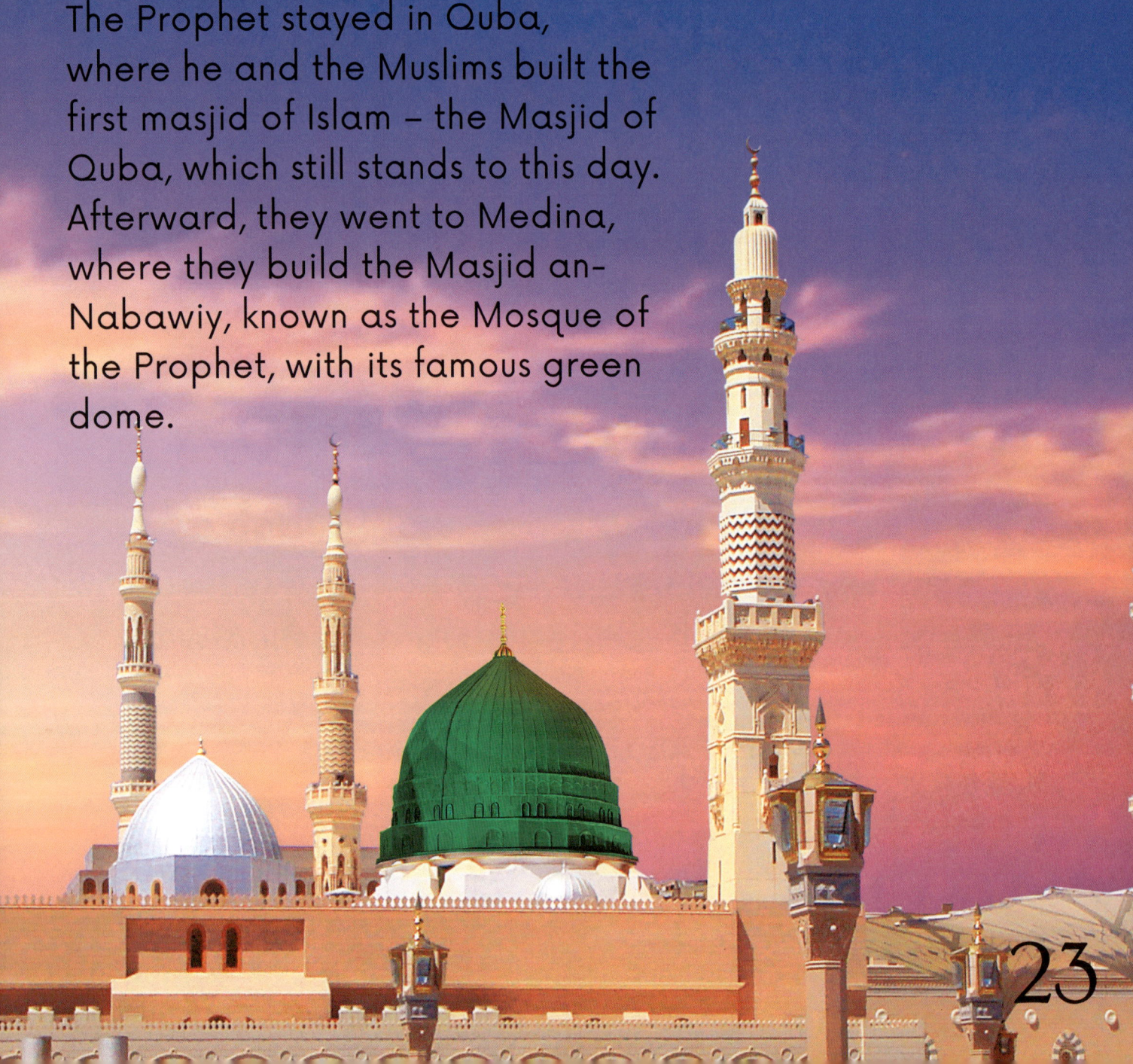

Muhammad Peace and Blessings of Allah upon him

Masjid an-Nabawiy is one of the places Muslims usually visit when they go on Umrah to the holy places in Mecca and Medina.

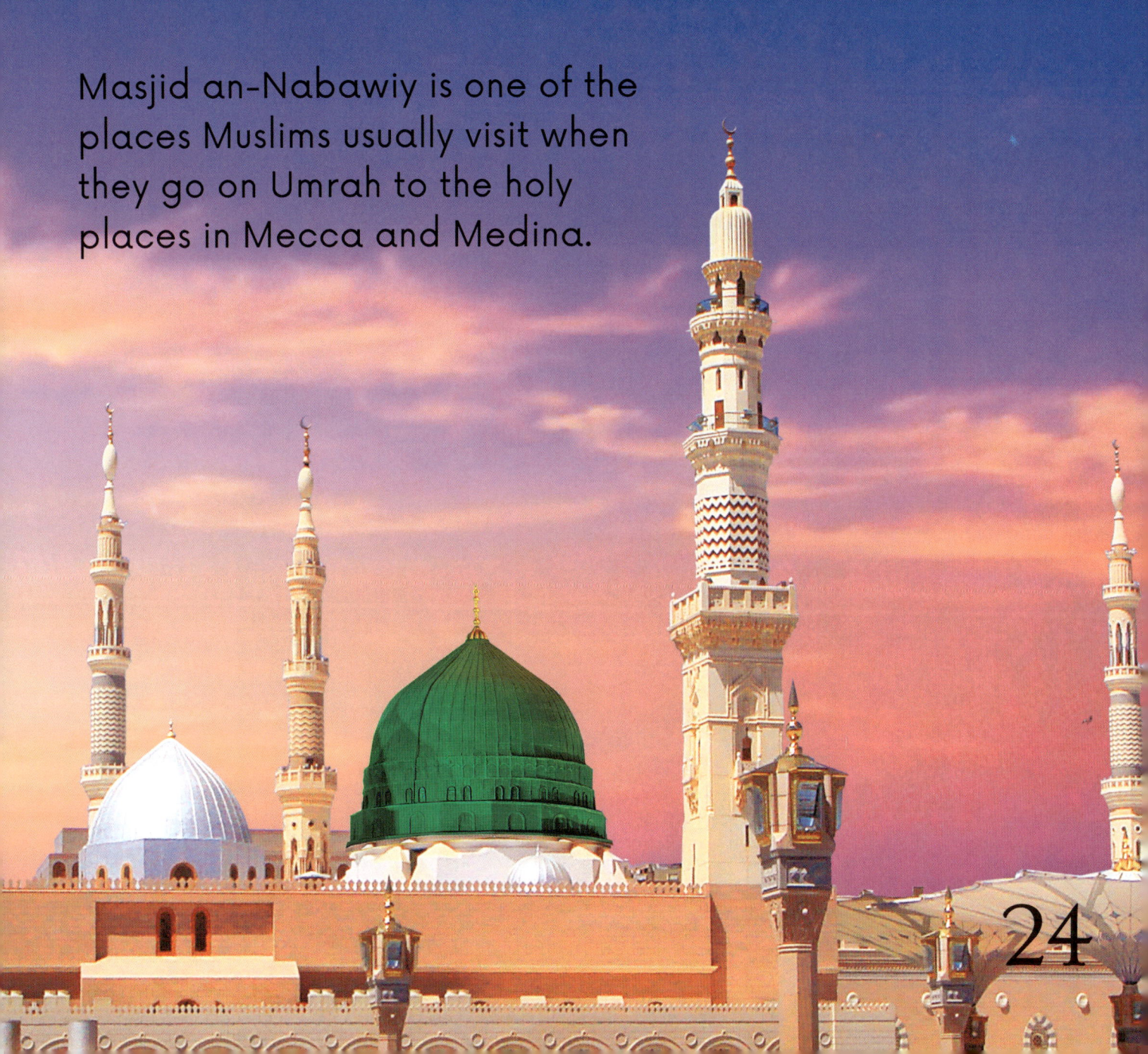

Muhammad Peace and Blessings of Allah upon him

After some years of peace in Medina, the Messenger (peace and blessings of Allah be upon him) decided to visit Mecca to go to the Kaaba and circle it in Tawaf. But the enemies of Islam who had power in Mecca did not want him to visit the Kaaba and did not let him.

Muhammad Peace and Blessings of Allah upon him

So the Prophet (peace and blessings of Allah be upon him) signed a peace treaty with them at al-Hudaybiyah, to stop the fighting for ten years, during which time the people would be safe and could do and believe as they wanted.

Muhammad Peace and Blessings of Allah upon him

After some time, the enemies of Islam in Mecca broke the treaty, so the Messenger (peace and blessings of Allah be upon him) headed towards them with a great army and won Mecca for the Muslims. He then removed the idols and statues from the Kaaba.

Muhammad Peace and Blessings of Allah upon him

The Prophet Muhammad (peace and blessings of Allah upon him) undertook his last visit to the Kaaba, in the year 10 A.H. In this visit, the Prophet would show the Muslims how to perform the fifth pillar of Islam, the Hajj. This Hajj was also the Prophet's first and last Hajj.

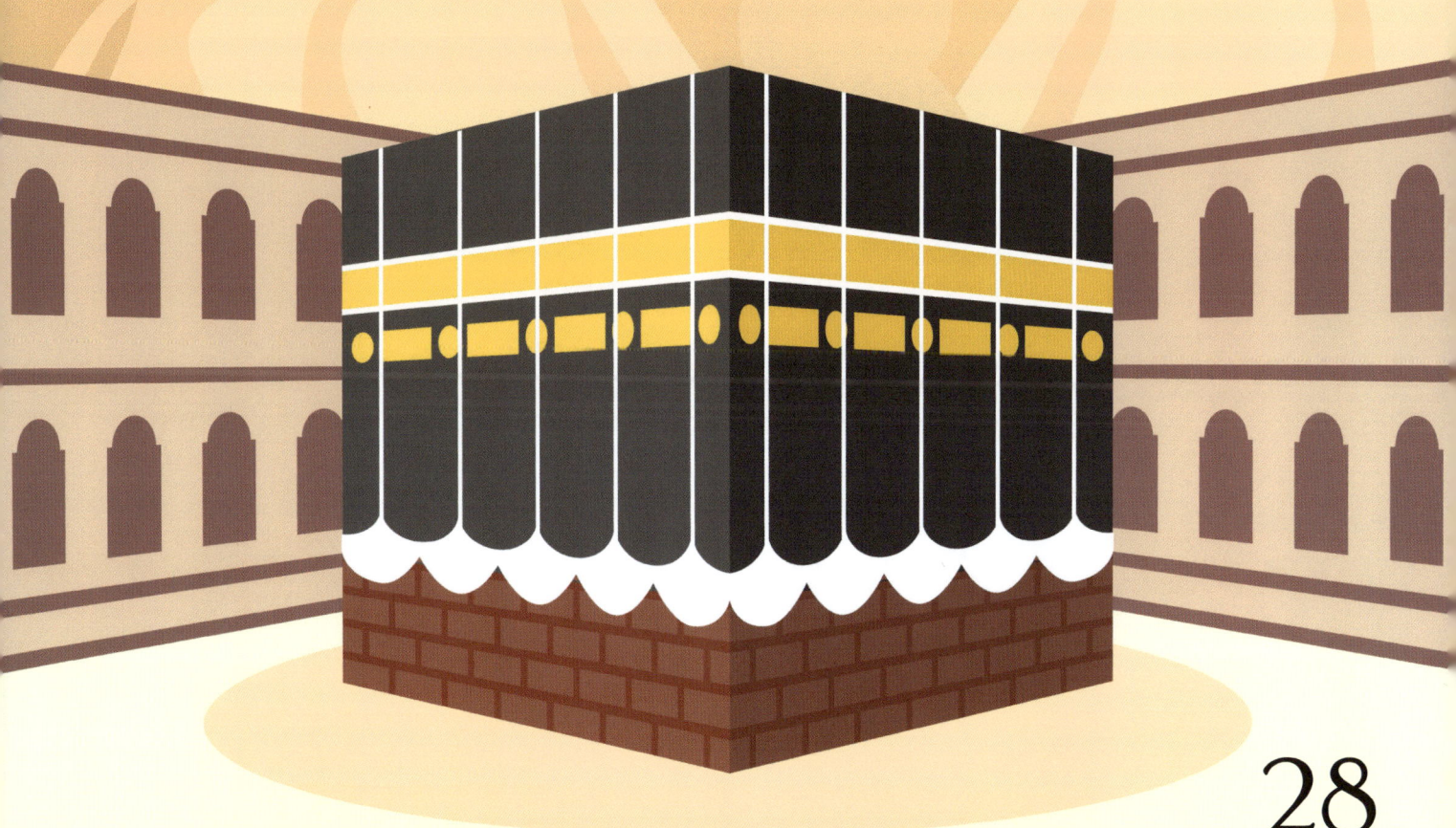

Muhammad Peace and Blessings of Allah upon him

Eleven years after traveling to Medina, in the month of Safar, the Messenger of Allah (peace and blessings of Allah be upon him) fell sick. When the pain became too much, he told Abu Bakr (may Allah be pleased with him) to lead the people in prayer. In the month of Rabee' al-Awwal, his sickness became worse, and the Prophet (peace and blessings of Allah be upon him) died.

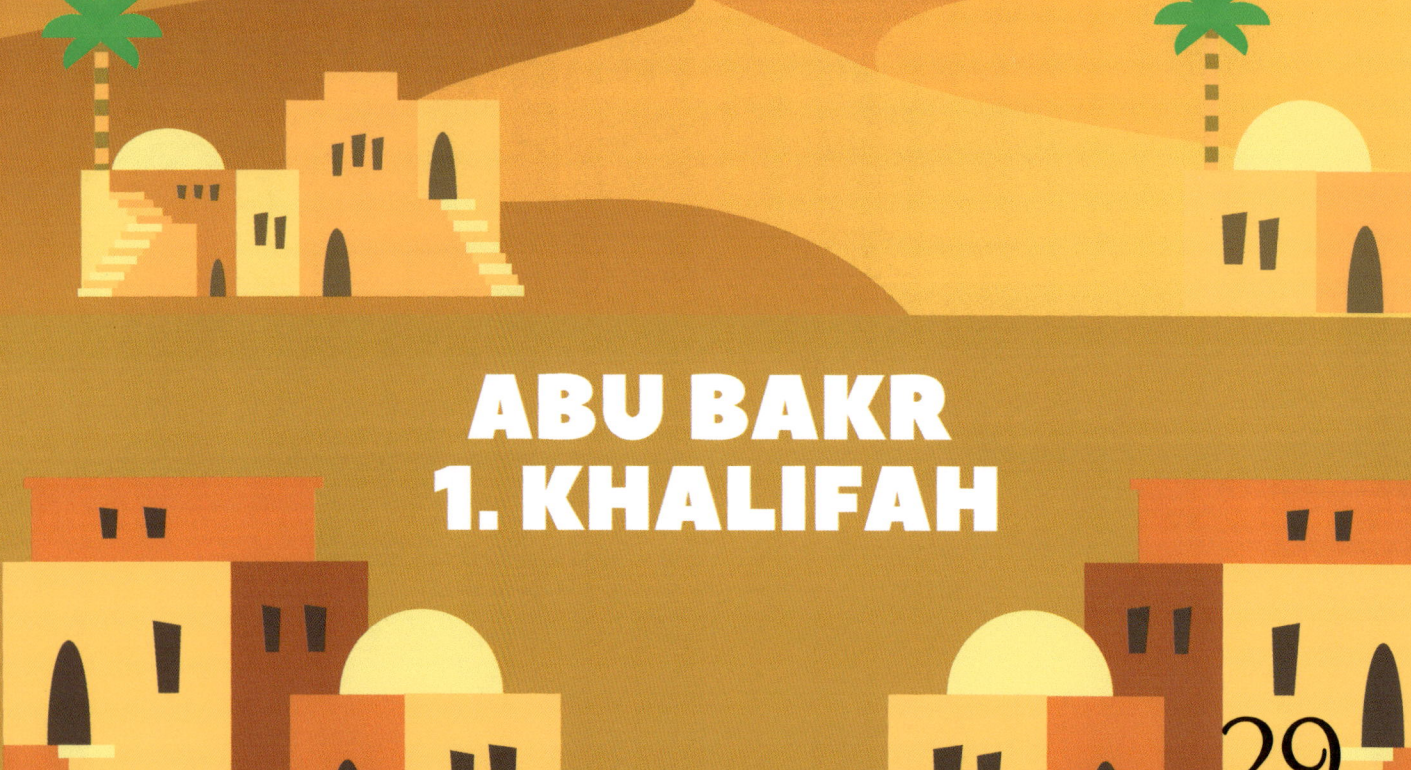

ABU BAKR
1. KHALIFAH

Muhammad Peace and Blessings of Allah upon him

Though the Messenger died, Allah declared that the religion he brought would stay through the Quran and the hearts of rightly-guided people until the Day of Resurrection. The Muslims chose Abu Bakr (may Allah be pleased with him) to lead them as their Khalifah and Imam, and Islam has continued to be taught and practiced ever since.

ABU BAKR
1. KHALIFAH

31

PROPHET MUSA ASKING TO SEE ALLAH

31

Prophet Musa asking to see Allah

"And when Musa (Moses) came at the time and place appointed by Us, and his Lord (Allah) spoke to him, he said: "O my Lord! Show me (Yourself), that I may look upon You." Allah said: "You cannot see Me, but look upon the mountain; if it stands still in its place then you shall see Me."

Prophet Musa asking to see Allah

"So when his Lord appeared to the mountain, He made it collapse to dust, and Musa (Moses) fell down unconscious. Then when he recovered his senses he said: "Glory be to You, I turn to You in repentance and I am the first of the believers." (Surah Al Araf; 143)

Prophet Musa asking to see Allah

"Our creator Allah has told us that no one can see Him in this world. Even Prophet Musa (peace be upon him), one of our greatest messengers, could not see Allah.

In Surah Al Araf, he asked Allah if he could see Him, and Allah told him instead to look at a mountain. Allah would show Himself to that mountain instead. When Allah revealed Himself to the mountain, the mountain crumbled to dust. That is because Allah is too great for His creation, human or mountain, to behold. When the mountain crumbled, the Prophet Musa fainted, and when he awoke, he asked Allah for forgiveness.

Prophet Musa asking to see Allah

"Prophet Mohammed (peace and blessings of Allah be upon him) could not see Allah. When Aisha, the wife of the Prophet (peace and blessings of Allah be upon him), was asked by Masruq if the Prophet had seen Allah, she replied: "My hair is standing on end because of what you have asked! Whoever tells you that Muhammad saw his Lord (Allah) has lied!" (Muslim, Volume 1, Hadith no. 337 & 339)

Prophet Musa asking to see Allah

"The Prophet himself admitted that he had never seen Allah. When Abu Dharr asked the Prophet (peace and blessings of Allah be upon him) if he had seen his Lord, the Prophet replied: "There was only light. How could I see Him?" (Muslim, Volume 1, Hadith no. 341)

Of course, Allah is not a light. What the Prophet was referring to is Allah's veil – or His covering, which is light. (Muslim, Volume 1, Hadith no. 343).

Prophet Musa asking to see Allah

"If Prophet Muhammad (peace and blessings of Allah be upon him) and the other prophets before him could not see Allah, then surely those who claim
that they have seen Allah must be mistaken.

As Allah says in the Quran: "Eyes cannot catch Him but He catches all eyes..." (6;103)

38

THE STORY OF THE GARDENS OF SHEBA

38

The Story of the Gardens of Sheba

Ibn Kathir wrote in his Tafsir that a long time ago, before the birth of Prophet Isa (Jesus) (peace be upon him), Yemen's land was home to a wealthy and powerful people of Sheba.

The Story of the Gardens of Sheba

They lived in a large city called Ma'aarib. There, they worked very hard to build great things, like orchards full of fruit trees and a dam that held back a river of water from flooding their homes.

The Story of the Gardens of Sheba

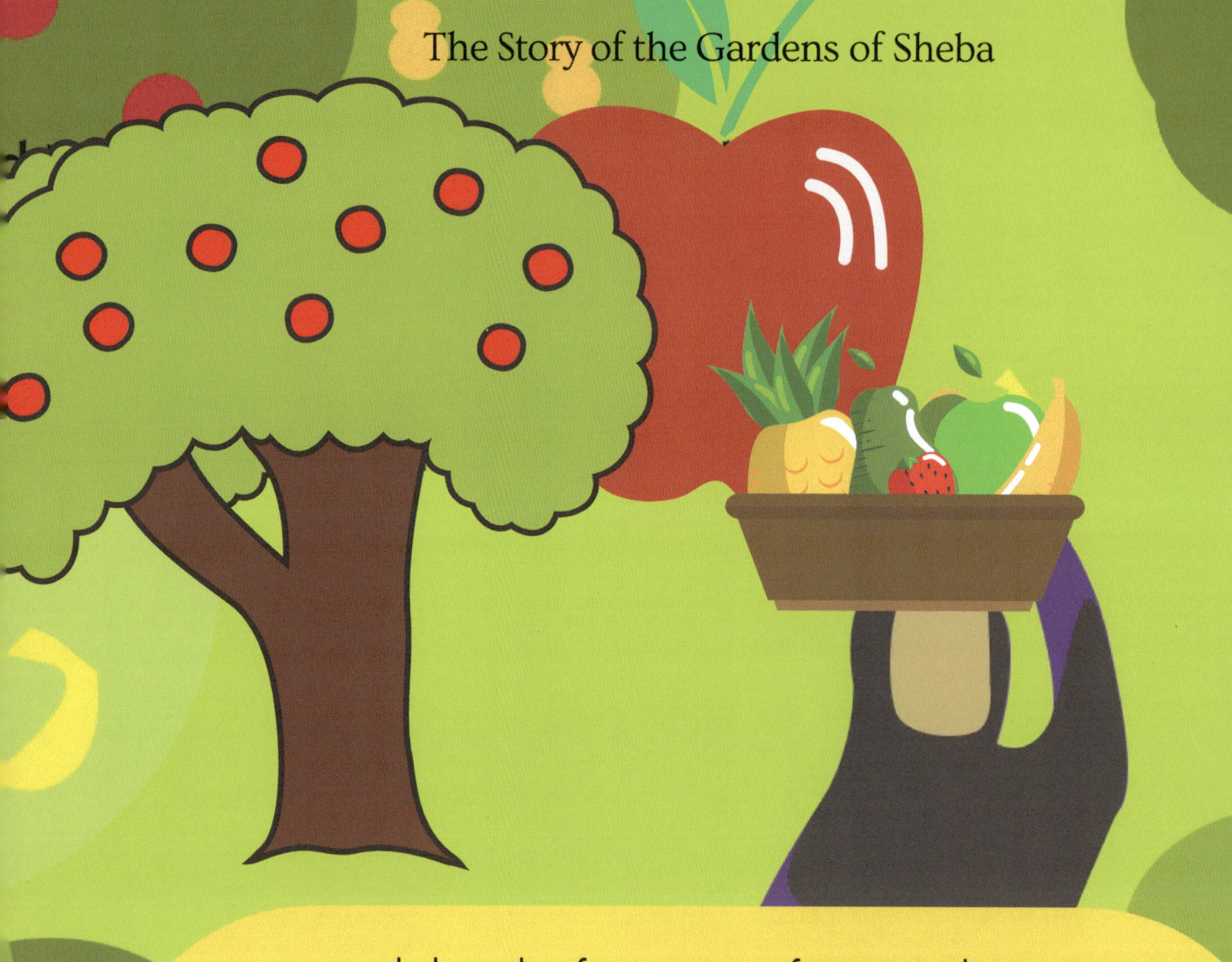

It was said that the fruit trees of Ma'aarib were so bountiful that a woman could walk beneath the trees carrying an empty basket on her head and emerge with a basket full of fruits. She would not need to stop and pick the fruit. They would fall from the trees, ripe and ready to eat.

The Story of the Gardens of Sheba

The city and its residents enjoyed many such blessings. They were even said to be free from the annoyances of flies and mosquitos. The town had good weather year-round, and the people were healthy. These blessings were all due to Allah's kindness and generosity, for which He told them to be thankful to Him alone. But the people of Ma'aarib did not listen to Allah. They did not thank him for the favors and blessings they enjoyed and instead became arrogant. Instead of worshipping Allah, they worshipped the sun and wrongly thanked it for their good fortune.

The Story of the Gardens of Sheba

Because they did not thank Allah and did not pray to Him alone, Allah punished the people of Ma'aarib by sending large rats that made holes in the dam.

The Story of the Gardens of Sheba

Then Allah sent heavy rain and floods. The floodwater overwhelmed the dam, which was weakened by the rats' holes, and it broke. All the water poured into the city and destroyed everything in its path: orchards, buildings, markets, and temples.

The Story of the Gardens of Sheba

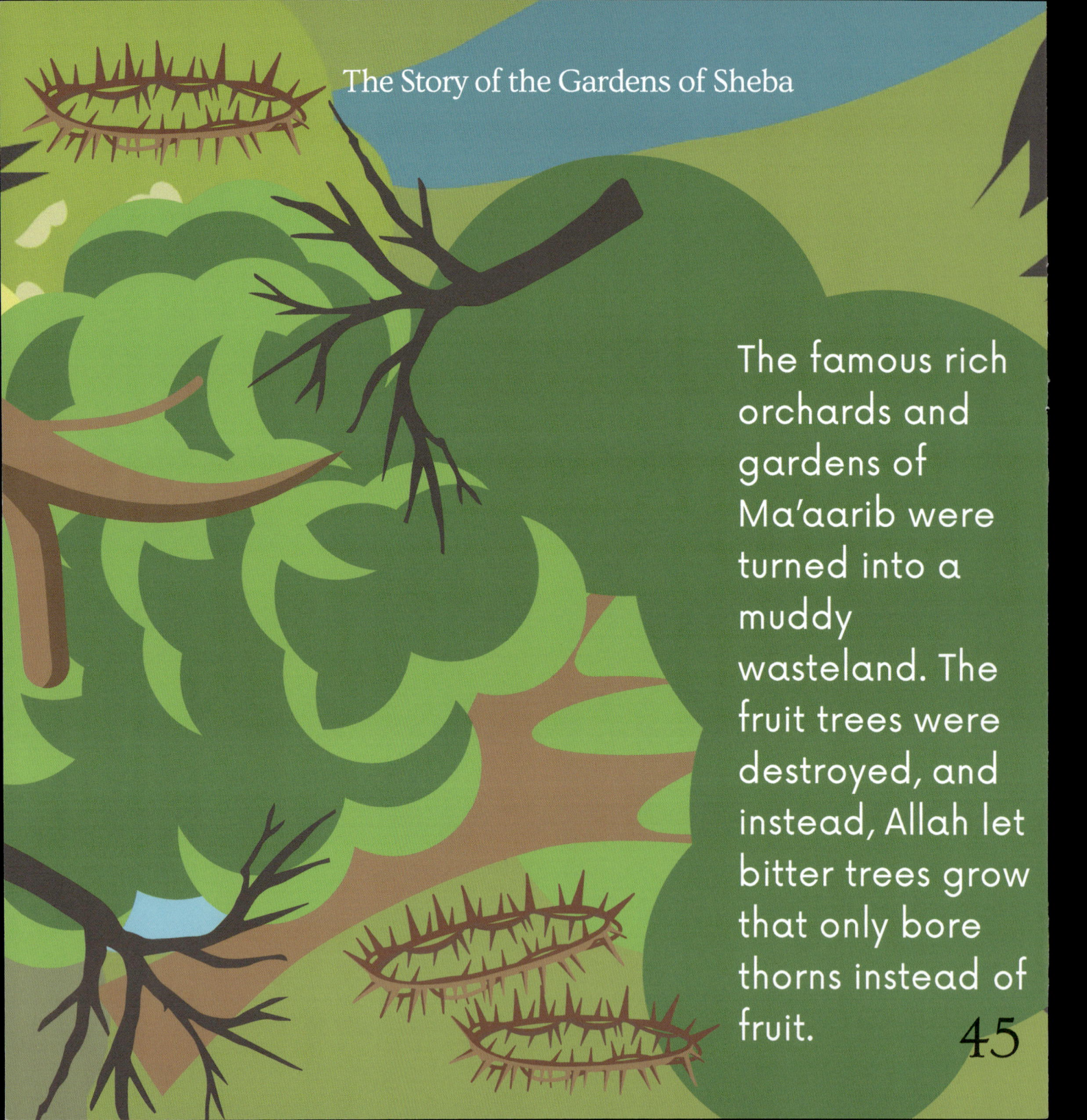

The famous rich orchards and gardens of Ma'aarib were turned into a muddy wasteland. The fruit trees were destroyed, and instead, Allah let bitter trees grow that only bore thorns instead of fruit.

The Story of the Gardens of Sheba

This punishment of the people of Ma'aarib teaches us that we must always remember to thank Allah for everything He has given us and pray to Him alone.

Thank you for choosing to buy this book -
I appreciate it!
If you find it useful, then please consider leaving a review on Amazon.
It would help me a lot.

You can sign up with your e-mail address on my website to find out when new books are being released and get FREE audiobooks, e-books, and other educational resources! I am still looking for reviewers for my new book about anger management in Islam for children.

go to:
http://www.islamicbooks.shop/

Printed in Great Britain
by Amazon

58782237R00030